Pocket Prayers

100 Scriptures and Prayers

Yolanda D. Turner

nubegining55@gmail.com

P. O. Box 303
Tanner, AL

NU Beginnings, LLC

Editing by Victoria Griggs

Cover and Interior Design by Victoria Griggs

Unless otherwise noted, all scripture is quoted from the New International Version (NIV)

ISBN 979-8-6574336-3-0

Printed in the United States of America

First Edition 14 13 12 11 10 / 10 9 8 7 6 5 4 3 2 1

*This Book of Prayers
Belongs To*

_____

ACKNOWLEDGEMENTS   *9*

FOREWORD   *11*

INTRODUCTION   *24*

I. RELATIONSHIP WITH GOD   *27*

ACCEPTING SALVATION   28
ACKNOWLEDGEMENT   28
ADMIRATION   29
BACKSLIDDEN STATE   29
COMMITMENT   30
COMMITMENT FOR THE AGING   30
CONFESSION   31
CONFESSION OF FAITH   31
DEMONSTRATION OF LOVE   32
DWELL WITHIN ME   32
FOR REPENTANCE   33
GIVING YOUR CARES TO GOD   33
GOD WILL FIGHT ON YOUR BEHALF   34
GOD WILL FINISH WHAT HE STARTED IN YOU   34
GOD'S PROMISES   35
GOD'S SPOKEN WORD   35
HIDDEN SINS   36
IDENTITY IN GOD   36
LIFE WORTHY OF SALVATION   37
NO CONDEMNATION   37
RECOMMITMENT   38

RECONCILIATION   38
REFUGE AND SAFETY   39
RESTORATION   39
SALVATION   40
SAVING GRACE   40
SEEKING GOD   41
THE LOVE OF THE FATHER   41
TRUST   42

II. SPIRITUAL GROWTH 43

ABUNDANTLY GIVING   44
ACCOUNTABLE LIVING   44
CONTROL OF THE TONGUE   45
DIRECTION OF THE HOLY SPIRIT   45
DISCERNING YOUR WILL   46
EARTHLY POSSESSIONS THAT HINDER   46
ENDURING FRUIT   47
EVALUATION OF MY FAITH   47
FASTING   48
FOOLISH WAYS   49
FOR RIGHTEOUS LIVING   50
FREE FROM WORLDLY THINKING   50
GOD'S UNDENIABLE POWER   51
GODLY CORRECTION   51
GREATER ANOINTING   52
GUIDANCE   52
HONORING THE SABBATH DAY   53
MAKING GOOD CHOICES   53
MEEKNESS IN BEAUTY   54
NEW BEGINNINGS   54

OUR NATION 55
PRAYING WITHOUT CEASING 55
PRIORITY OF MINISTRY 56
REAPING AND SOWING 56
SAFEGUARDING THE GOSPEL IN THE HEART 57
SPIRITUAL DISCERNMENT 57
SPIRITUAL GROWTH 58
SPIRITUAL UNITY 58
STABILITY 59
STEWARDSHIP IN MINISTRY 59
STILLNESS 60
STRENGTHEN YOUR FAITH 60
THE GOODNESS OF GOD WITHIN ME 61
SUBMISSION TO HIS WILL 61
WISDOM, UNDERSTANDING, AND KNOWLEDGE 62
WISE LIVING 62

III. RELATIONSHIPS 63

CHILDREN SAFETY 64
DISARMING CONFLICT 64
DIVINE ORDER 65
EDIFICATION 65
EXPOSING DECEIT 66
FAMILY SERVITUDE 66
FOR THE ELDERLY 67
FORGIVENESS 67
FORGIVENESS AND LOVE 68
GODLY INFLUENCE 68
GRATEFUL NATION 69
LOVING OTHERS 69

LYING LIPS AND DECEIT   70
MARRIAGE   70
PROTECTION FOR MISSIONARIES   71
REARING YOUR CHILDREN IN CHRIST   71
THE BROKEN-HEARTED   72
TO LOVE MY ENEMIES   72
WISE COUNSEL   73

IV. OVERCOMING ADVERSITY   75

ADDITION   76
AVENGE WICKEDNESS   76
BEING VICTORIOUS DURING TRIALS   77
DELIVERANCE   77
DELIVERANCE FROM ANGER   78
DELIVERANCE FROM MY ENEMIES   78
HEALING   79
PATIENCE FOR THE HURTING   79
PEACEFUL   80
PREVAILING AGAINST TEMPTATION   80
RESCUE   81
STEADFASTNESS IN TRIAL   81
STRENGTHENED TO OVERCOME   82
TEMPER   82
THE WEAK IN FAITH   83

THE LORD'S PRAYER   85

PRAYER LOG   86

Acknowledgments

"The Intercessor Christ Jesus"

*Who then is the one who condemns? No one. Christ Jesus who
died, more than that, who was raised to life, is at the right hand
of God and is also interceding for us.*
Romans 8:34

AND TO ALL THE

Prayer Warriors
Thank you, for standing in the gap by interceding in prayer.

Foreword

It is my honor to be presenting this foreword of scriptures and prayers written by those who have been instrumental in my spiritual growth. By the promptings and leading of the Holy Spirit, I have selected a few of many people who support my life of prayer, spiritual teachings, and Godly accountability. I pray that you will find the needed encouragement from the prayers shared by these anointed prayer warriors to include the prayers offered by the Author. May these prayers be a timely source of hope, strength, and direction in your time of need.

My mother was a praying woman who prayed nonstop. She would wake up praying, she prayed throughout the day while doing household chores, and she would pray with us at night before bedtime. She prayed all the time. When I think of an image of a person praying without ceasing, I think of my mother and my wife, Yolanda Turner.

As long as I have known Yolanda, she has always prayed. She learned to pray through the many hardships and trails that life brought her way. As a two-time divorcee and a single mother of two young girls, she had ample opportunity and need for prayer. As I watched her struggle to raise and provide for her daughters, working a forty-hour a week job, volunteering at many school functions, coaching her daughters' cheerleading team, working faithfully in the church as a youth leader, and active choir member, I also watched her grow in the Word of God and how her prayers changed spiritually. Her prayers went from pleading, to begging, to attempting to negotiate with God, to a strong and powerful prayer warrior that defeated any foe that challenged her.

Her victory in prayer came from praying the Word of God. She understood that God's Word would stand forever, He would honor his Word, and His Word would not come back void. So, she learned to pray the promises that God's Word guaranteed to those who believed. She stood on the Word of God and all its promises by faith claiming them all with "Yes and Amen."

Foreword

I am a witness to her unapologetic approach to her faith in prayer. She has prayed for many people in public including supermarkets, department stores, gas stations, rest areas, doctor appointments, anywhere; the location is never a hinderance for her. She is so in tune with the Holy Spirit that she does not hesitate to approach a person and say, "Can I pray for you?" What is amazing about her fearless act of praying for people in public is that they all always say to her, "How did you know? I have never told anyone." She would reply, "God revealed it to me through the Holy Spirit." Many of them would just cry after her statement, and she reminds them all that God loves them and that He has not forgotten about them. With a big smile, she would leave them with these words "He knows you by name, and He has you in the palms of His hands."

Our blended family of four daughters, ages from 27 to 35 years old, and our four grandsons, ages from 8 to 18 years old, is the beneficiary of Yolanda's continuous prayers. There has not been one situation that has occurred within our family that was not resolved through prayer. Our family has faced every situation imaginable, and as parents, we did not always know how to best handle those situations, but we knew how to pray and proclaim God's promises over our marriage, our family, our jobs, our children and their educational challenges, over our community, over our relationship with each other, and the list goes on. Prayer has been the most important factor that has kept us strong in our faith and kept us close to our Lord and Savior.

Foreword

I am excited about *Pocket Prayers* because I know that this book will help strengthen your prayers. It is designed to teach you how to pray God's Word in every situation. Yolanda provides 100 scriptures and a personal prayer for each scripture to illustrate how easy it is to pray the scriptures. One of Yolanda's favorite sayings is "God will do what He said He would do!" So, whether you are learning to pray for the first time or you are an experienced prayer warrior, *Pocket Prayers* will definitely help increase your knowledge of God's Word and strengthen your prayer life, which will allow you to enjoy many more victories through your prayers.

Father God, I pray for everyone that uses these prayers contained in this *Pocket Prayers* book, that they will find strength and wisdom in every situation that they face in life. I pray that *Pocket Prayers* will open up the eyes of their hearts to your promises and enlighten their minds to your Word so that they can experience many victories through their prayers. Let them grow spiritually and let their faith be strengthen as they continually proclaim Your Word in their prayers. In Jesus' Name, Amen!

Evangelist – Teacher Gregory D. Turner

Father, I am truly grateful for Your Love for us. I am so thankful for the gift of prayer! It is our way to communicate with You on an intimate level. Just to know that we have an Audience with You gives us hope. Your Word instructs us to pray without ceasing. And knowing that You never slumber nor sleep, gives us an assurance that we can call on You at any time. You said we can cast our cares on You because You care for us. You have so many promises in Your Word for us and by praying Your Word, we know we will receive Your Will for our lives. I pray for every soul that will encounter this book. I pray their lives will be forever changed. I pray they will experience You and Your Power like never before. I pray every reader of this book will have a transformed prayer life and a renewed hunger for Your Word. And finally, I pray that You will enlarge Yolanda's territory and increase her borders and God; bless her indeed! Amen.

Esther Garrett

Heavenly Father, thank You for my Sister in Christ, Yolanda! I am forever grateful for her obedience to listen to Your voice and the birth of her ministry. She has been relentless in her passion for serving and sharing the joys of Your Word. I pray that as she continues her journey, continue to guide her, and impart in her the wisdom and compassion necessary. For everywhere the soles of her feet shall tread, You have already made a provision for her. Lord, thank You, for my friend! We shall offer You the constant praise and glory as we go forth and do Your Will, Amen.

Beverly K Johnson

Heavenly Father, I ask you that when I am wrong, show me the condition of my heart and correct it to reflect You and Your Will. If the other person is wrong, show them as well and correct their heart. Help me to be gracious even when I am right and even more humble when I am wrong so that an agreement can be reached in a way that will bring You glory. In Jesus' Name I pray, Amen.

Holy Shut-up Prayer
Minister Victoria Griggs

Father, in the name of Jesus, I give You praise because You are good. I thank You Lord for Your mercies and Your grace, which we are standing in right now. May You continue to uplift the readers and give them the ability to move forth towards the kingdom assignment that You have established for them. May You encourage them in their seasons of discouragement, may You lift them in their times of turmoil, and may You push them toward purpose in every single day that You allow them to exist. May favor go before them, goodness and mercy follow them, and may Christ be in them, which is the hope of glory. Remind them that they are Overcomers by the blood of the lamb and by the Word of their testimony. And they should love not their lives even unto death in Jesus' Name, Amen

Pastor Daryl Arnold
Overcoming Believers Church
Knoxville, TN

Foreword

May God bless the hearts and minds of every person who picks up this book. May He bless them as they read these words and focus on those things that are true, honest, just, pure, and lovely. May they allow the truths of God's Word and the power of His love to permeate their minds as they take every thought captive to the obedience of Christ. May every inclination of their hearts, every desire, every disappointment, and every difficult circumstance be met with His perfect peace. And may every mouth be filled with total praise, Amen.

Dr. Danella 'Dee' Knight

Father, I thank You for Your tender mercies and Your grace. You have given us many tools of study so that we can be closer to You. Help us to be the Children of God who reach out to the hurting and needy. Amen.

Kelly Overton

Lord Father, as this next book is published, I pray your Holy Spirit will anoint it with power, with healing, with joy, and with Your peace. I pray also that Yolanda and her family would be blessed as You send forth Your Word through her. It is in the powerful name of Jesus and all for His Glory, Amen.

Jami Tomlin

Foreword

Father, we thank You for Yolanda, the author of this book, in how You are using her as a vessel to bring about victory through prayer. As persons read this book, may the Word of God and prayer become a reality in their life. May You be revealed as Savior, provider, healer, sustainer, and deliverer in this book.

Your word says in **1 John 5:14, 15** "And this is the confidence that we have in Him, that, if we ask any thing according to His Will, He heareth us: And if we know that He hear us, whatsoever we ask, we know that we have the petitions that we desired of Him".

We thank You for confirming Your Word in the lives of those who read this book. We thank You for the lives that will be saved and changed through this book. We thank You for the marriages that will be encouraged and strengthened through this book. May this book bring glory to Your name! In Jesus' Name we pray, Amen!

Pastor Troy Garner
The Fellowship of Faith Church
Huntsville and Madison, AL

Father God, we ask You to come into our weary hearts with compassion. We pray to You knowing that as we wait on You for answered prayer that in due season, we will hear Your voice and You will answer our plea. We always remember that the darkest hour is just before dawn. We all encounter hard times, but we must know that You will never leave us or forsake us. You are carrying us when we do not feel like getting out of the bed. God you are there when we have no one to whom we can talk. God you are there even when we cannot hear You. All we must do is call the name of Jesus! When we have done all we can do and do not have strength to carry on, we will just stand and know You are God. Amen!

Lora P. Smiley

Jesus defeated the enemy when He died on the cross. We now fight from victory not for victory. **Colossians 2:15**

Father God help me to put on the spiritual armor that You use to protect me from harm and help me stand before the enemy. Help me to tie the belt of truth around my waist and protect my heart with the breastplate of righteousness.

Put on the full armor of God, so that you will be able to stand firm against the schemes of the devil. **Ephesians 6:11**

Let me place upon my feet the preparation of the gospel of peace, so that I can share the good news with others, and help me hold in my hands the shield of faith which can put out the flaming darts of the wicked one.

I pray that You will equip my brothers and sisters around the world with the Armor of God and teach them how to use the pieces. I pray for the strength we need to fight our battles. You said, "No weapon formed against us will ever prosper." I ask in Jesus' name that You fulfill this in our lives. Amen.

Our prayers matter to God. They are not just empty words that we are shouting into the sky. Prayers break down walls.

Prayer for Spiritual Battle
LaBrina Grose

 *Foreword*

Lord Jesus, I worship You, I adore You, I magnify You
You are the head and You guide my hands and feet.
Lord Jesus, I surrender to You.
Allow me to change this world and bring Heaven to earth.
I want to walk like You, see like You, touch like You.
Instruct me and teach in that path I should go.
I thank You Lord for choosing me to pour out Your Spirit.
I thank You Lord for giving me the power and authority to
trample on any snake or scorpions and nothing shall harm me.
Thank You, Lord for blessing me beyond favor,
and allow me to be a blessing to someone today.
Touch my tongue, as it will be like a pen of a writer and pierce
someone hearts today.
Lord please forgive me and our world of anything that is not of
You.
I humble myself to You Lord.
I thank You God the Father for making me in Your image.
I thank You Lord Jesus for dying for my sins of yesterday.
I thank You Holy Spirit for guiding my steps of tomorrow.
In Jesus' Name I pray, Amen.

Pastor Corey Jewell-Taylor
Church of Destiny
Madison, AL

Heavenly Father, we come before You with a praise on our lips and gratefulness in our hearts. Lord we thank You for allowing us another day in your Holy presence. Father God, we love You and we praise You Lord. We praise You not only for what You are doing in the lives of Your people, but we simply praise You for who You are. You are Jehovah Jireh, our provider. Thank You, Lord, for always providing for us. Thank You, Lord, for Your mercy, Your grace, and Your loving kindness toward us. Lord, thank You for Your hand of protection over our lives. Lord, we praise You and appreciate You for keeping us safe from all hurt, harm, and danger.

Lord, thank You for blessing us individually and collectively. Thank You for blessing our homes, our families, our spouses, our children, our relatives, our friends, and our possessions. Lord, we thank You for the peace that we have through You that comforts us in the midst of adversity. Lord, we thank You for being our joy, our strength, and the assurance of knowing that we can lean on You whenever we are troubled. Father God, thank You for being a deliverer, for Your Word says, "many are the afflictions of the righteous, but You will deliver us from them all." Thank You, Lord, for being a way maker, a promise keeper, and a light in darkness. Thank You, Lord, for being a restorer, a healer, and a comforter. Lord, thank You for new mercies every day. Lord, we thank You for being our great hope for a declining nation, and Lord, we thank You for being an encourager through Your Word. Lord, we thank You for being a Great and awesome GOD, and we thank You for being a gracious God.

We praise You and thank You for transforming our hearts and minds to conform to Your Will and Your Way. Father God, we thank You for Your gift of eternal life and Salvation through Your son Jesus Christ. God, we praise You, we honor You, and we give You glory for the countless blessings You have bestowed upon us daily. Lord God, we offer this prayer of thanksgiving to You, and we anticipate in faith the manifestation of Your Word and blessings. It is in the matchless name of Jesus' we pray, Amen!

Evangelist Gloria Maxwell

 *Introduction*

Pocket Prayers is a collection of scriptural prayers designed to be carried in your pocket or purse. This small yet powerful book offers on-the-spot prayers when life's challenges and adversities arise throughout the busyness of your day. *Pocket Prayers* includes timely scriptural prayers that equip you to declare God's Word to center your thoughts and prayers on the promises of God! *Pocket Prayers* is not a replacement for the Holy Bible, but it is the perfect book to have in your pocket for urgent, spontaneous prayers!

Prayer is a direct line to God used to submit our hearts and thoughts to GOD with honest dialogue about our fears, disappointments, human weakness, and sudden attacks of afflictions from the works of Satan. Seeking God's Will in every situation should be our first priority in prayer.

God has given us the most powerful weapon for spiritual warfare and that is praying God's Word, which enables us to overcome spiritual forces of evil, offense, grief, and mental torment just to name a few. God commands us to pray continuously in **(1 Thessalonians 5:17)** so that we can stand against every unforeseen attack and ultimately conquering all the evil plots assigned to us.

Anything that Satan uses to steal, harm, destroy or kill needs to be defeated by the power of God's Word through prayer. We need anointed prayer warriors interceding on the behalf of our love ones and for the unbeliever by the leading of the Holy Spirit.

We need prayers that will keep us rooted in Christ Jesus in times of conflict and trials. We need prayers for Salvation and unity throughout the world. We are all called to pray! Do not take prayer lightly for it carries tremendous spiritual power that enables us to break the strongholds of sin. Prayer can change the outcome of Satan's evil plots that are meant to destroy God's people.

For our struggle is not against flesh and blood, but against the rulers, against the authorities, against the powers of this dark world and against the spiritual forces of evil in the heavenly realms.
Ephesians 6:12

Do not be anxious about anything, but in every situation, by prayer and petition, with thanksgiving, present your requests to God. And the peace of God, which transcends all understanding, will guard your hearts and your minds in Christ Jesus.
Philippians 4:6-7

And pray in the Spirit on all occasions with all kinds of prayers and request. With this in mind, be alert and always keep on praying for all the Lord's people.
Ephesians 6:18

My prayer is not that you take them out of the world but that you protect them from the evil one.
John 17:15

Relationship

with God

Accepting Salvation

Scripture

The Lord is not slow in keeping his promise, as some understand slowness. Instead he is patient with you, not wanting anyone to perish, but everyone to come to repentance.
2 Peter 3:9

Scriptural Prayer

Oh Lord, I thank You for Your promise of Salvation and patience toward us all. You were not willing to let anyone perish but to come to You through repentance. I fully surrender my life to You and accept Your promise of Salvation. In Jesus' Name, Amen.

Acknowledgement

Scripture

But from everlasting to everlasting the LORD's love is with those who fear him, and his righteousness with their children's children with those who keep his covenant and remember to obey his precepts.
Psalm 103:17-18

Scriptural Prayer:

Heavenly Father, thank You for Your everlasting love that is poured out on those who acknowledge You, reverence You, and keep Your commandments. They shall inherit the guaranteed promises of righteousness for themselves and their children's children. In Jesus' Name, Amen.

Admiration

Scripture

The LORD commanded us to obey all these decrees and to fear the LORD our God, so that we might always prosper and be kept alive, as is the case today.

Deuteronomy 6:24

Scriptural Prayer

Father God, I reverence You with great admiration and because of this, I will obey and keep all Your commands that I might find favor and long-life in Your sight. In Jesus' Name, Amen.

Backslidden State

Scripture

But as soon as they were at rest, they again did what was evil in your sight. Then you abandoned them to the hand of their enemies so that they ruled over them. And when they cried out to you again, you heard from heaven, and in your compassion, you delivered them time after time.

Nehemiah 9:28

Scripture Prayer

Heavenly Father, I acknowledge that so many times I have turned my back on You in my sinful, backslidden state. In times of despair, I cried out in repentance for Your help, and You answered my cries because of Your mercy towards me; You delivered me time after time. Give me a heart like Yours to forgive and have compassion for those who have hurt and rejected me. In Jesus' Name, Amen.

Commitment

Scripture

Therefore, my dear brothers and sisters, stand firm. Let nothing move you. Always give yourselves fully to the work of the Lord because you know that your labor in the Lord is not in vain.
1 Corinthians 15:58

Scriptural Prayer

Heavenly Father, You have equipped me through Your Holy Spirit, and You have given me many talents and skillsets not to be used in vain but for Kingdom building. Lord, remove any fears and deceitful motives trying to divert or stop me from completing my divine assignment to share with others the Good News of Your saving grace that is full of power, hope, peace, and everlasting love. In Jesus' Name, Amen.

Commitment for the Aging

Scripture

Even when I am old and gray, do not forsake me, my God, till I declare your power to the next generation, your mighty acts to all who are to come.
Psalm 71:18

Scriptural Prayer

Heavenly Father, even in my old age, up until my death, I will declare Your goodness and continue to be living proof of Your mighty acts for all to witness. In Jesus' Name, Amen.

Confession

Scripture

I said, "Have mercy on me, LORD; heal me, for I have sinned against you."

Psalm 41:4

Scriptural Prayer

Heavenly Father, I confess and repent for my sins. I repent for (Confess your sins). My sins caused me to disobey Your Word. Lord, have mercy on me; heal and restore me back to You. In Jesus' Name, Amen.

Confession of Faith

Scripture

If you declare with your mouth, "Jesus is Lord," and believe in your heart that God raised him from the dead, you will be saved. For it is with your heart that you believe and are justified, and it is with your mouth that you profess your faith and are saved.

Romans 10:9-10

Scriptural Prayer

Lord, I pray for Your forgiveness of all the sins that I have committed. I believe in my heart that You died on the cross for my sins and was resurrected from the grave. I confess with my mouth, that Jesus Christ is my Lord and Savior, and I believe by my faith that I am saved. In Jesus' Name, Amen.

Demonstration of Love

Scripture

But God demonstrates his own love for us in this: While we were still sinners, Christ died for us.

Romans 5:8

Scriptural Prayer

Heavenly Father, Your Son, Jesus Christ, carried all my sins to the cross at Calvary where He died for me. Even before I believed and loved Him, His unconditional love remained unmovable. The actions and promises of our Lord and Savior demonstrate His love, and He continues to be the greatest love ever known to mankind. In Jesus' Name, Amen.

Dwell Within Me

Scripture

Do you not know that your bodies are temples of the Holy Spirit, who is in you, whom you have received from God? You are not your own.

1 Corinthians 6:19

Scriptural Prayer

Heavenly Father, my body and soul belong to You. Lord, give me the power to avoid things that do not edify You, and keep my mind on things that are pure and righteous so that I do not defile my body and grieve the Holy Spirit. My body is a living temple created to fellowship with You in Spirit and truth. Remove any ungodly habits that cause separation from Your Spirit. In Jesus' Name, Amen.

For Repentance

Scripture

For troubles without number surround me; my sins have overtaken me, and I cannot see. They are more than the hairs of my head, and my heart fails within me.
Psalm 40:12

Scriptural Prayer

Oh Lord, heal and surround me with Your saving grace. I am consumed with the consequences of my sins; I repent for my wrongdoings. Cleanse my heart with the overflow of joy and peace that only You can give. Guide me safety back into Your marvelous light. In Jesus' Name, Amen.

Giving Your Cares to God

Scripture

Who of you by worrying can add a single hour to your life? Since you cannot do this very little thing, why do you worry about the rest?
Luke 12:25-26

Scriptural Prayer

Heavenly Father, I have life and everything I need in You. I cast all my burdens upon You; remove any anxiety that causes me to worry more than trusting in You. In Jesus' Name, Amen.

God Will Fight on Your Behalf

Scripture

The LORD will fight for you; you need only to be still.
Exodus 14:14

Scriptural Prayer

Oh Lord, the battle is not mine; it is Yours! I will remain in peace, firmly rooted in You. Thank You for being a wall of protection that surrounds me. In Jesus' Name, Amen.

God Will Finish What He Started in You

Scripture

Being confident of this, that he who began a good work in you will carry it on to completion until the day of Christ Jesus.
Philippians 1:6

Scriptural Prayer

Father God, it was my wrongful actions that opened the door to the consequences of my sins. In my guilt, I turned away from You, but Your watchful eye never abandoned me. Even though I broke your heart in my wrongdoings, You exposed them by correcting and restoring me back to your protective care. Lord, I know You will finish the works that You have started in me. Thank You for never giving up on me. In Jesus' Name, Amen.

God's Promises

Scripture

So is my word that goes out from my mouth: It will not return to me empty, but will accomplish what I desire and achieve the purpose for which it was sent.

Isaiah 55:11

Scriptural Prayer

Heavenly Father, Your Word accomplishes everything You command it to do. From the richest to the most powerful; to the poorest and most humble; to every person of every age Your promises are guaranteed, and Your judgments will be fulfilled according to Your Word. In Jesus' Name, Amen.

God's Spoken Word

Scripture

For he spoke, and it came to be; he commanded, and it stood firm.

Psalm 33:9

Scriptural Prayer

LORD, You spoke, and it came to be. You commanded, and it stood firm. Your spoken Word is a hedge of protection that binds up every principality and every spirit of wickedness. Your spoken promises stand firm to deliver me from every snare and danger that is assigned to destroy me. Your spoken commands are mighty in power and authority which is given to me to declare Your Word that disarms every weapon formed against me! Your Word will stand firmly forevermore. In Jesus' Name, Amen.

Hidden Sins

Scripture

"Who can hide in secret places so that I cannot see them?" declares the LORD. "Do not I fill heaven and earth?" declares the LORD.

Jeremiah 23:24

Scriptural Prayer

Heavenly Father, I know there are no earthly places hidden from Your sight or unspoken secrets concealed from Your hearing. Reveal my hidden sins that would cause me to fall destroying my precious soul. As your presence fills heaven and earth, occupy my heart for You are an all-knowing God, and I belong to You. In Jesus' Name, Amen.

Identity in God

Scripture

So God created mankind in his own image, in the image of God he created them; male and female he created them.

Genesis 1:27

Scriptural Prayer

Heavenly Father, I am Your masterpiece. You carefully and intentionally created me. You created me to be a reflection of Your beauty and love. You created me to be a light on the earth for Your glory. I thank You for creating me in Your image. In Jesus' Name, Amen.

Life Worthy of Salvation

Scripture

For I know that through your prayers and God's provision of the Spirit of Jesus Christ what has happened to me will turn out for my deliverance

Philippians 1:19

Scripture Prayer

Thank You, Heavenly Father, for the power of the Holy Spirit and the prayers of others that has given me the strength and courage to live a life worthy of my Salvation for which Christ died. In Jesus' Name, Amen.

No Condemnation

Scripture

For God did not send his Son into the world to condemn the world, but to save the world through him.

John 3:17

Scriptural Prayer

Our Father in Heaven, thank You for Your Son, Jesus, who came from heaven as a man living a humble existence to serve and to save a condemned world from eternal damnation. In Jesus' Name, Amen.

Recommitment

Scripture

I will give them a heart to know me, that I am the LORD. They will be my people, and I will be their God, for they will return to me with all their heart.

Jeremiah 24:7

Scriptural Prayer

Heavenly Father forgive me for turning away from You. I recommit myself back to You for my heart longs after You; I acknowledge You as my God, as You have always acknowledged me as Your child even when I denied You. Thank You for never abandoning me. In Jesus' Name, Amen.

Reconciliation

Scripture

Remember that at that time you were separate from Christ, excluded from citizenship in Israel and foreigners to the covenants of the promise, without hope and without God in the world; And in one body to reconcile both of them to God through the cross, by which he put to death their hostility.

Ephesian 2:12,16

Scriptural Prayer

Heavenly Father, if it had not been for Your Son dying on the cross, we would have been alienated from Your promises that were guaranteed to Your chosen people. Jesus' death on the cross established the reconciliation of mankind back to You making us Your people that can now live in unity and peace with You. In Jesus' Name, Amen.

Refuge and Safety

Scripture

He will cover you with his feathers, and under his wings you will find refuge; his faithfulness will be your shield and rampart. You will not fear the terror of night, nor the arrow that flies by day, nor the pestilence that stalks in the darkness, nor the plague that destroys at midday. A thousand may fall at your side, ten thousand at your right hand, but it will not come near you.
Psalm 91:4-7

Scriptural Prayer

Heavenly Father, You are my dwelling place. Your ever presence is my shield. I will fear no unforeseen harm or evil plots that are assigned to destroy me through sicknesses, fear, or lack for Your faithfulness will rescue me and Your everlasting love covers me. In Jesus' Name, Amen.

Restoration

Scripture

Return to your fortress, you prisoners of hope; even now I announce that I will restore twice as much to you.
Zechariah 9:12

Scriptural Prayer

Heavenly Father, You are my liberator. You are my fortress and my dwelling place where my hope is anchored. Thank You for restoring me exceedingly and above all that the enemy has taken from me. In Jesus' Name, Amen.

Salvation

Scripture

For my Father's will is that everyone who looks to the Son and believes in him shall have eternal life, and I will raise them up at the last day.

John 6:40

Scriptural Prayer

Heavenly Father, Your Will is that no one be lost but for all to come to believe that your Son, Jesus Christ is our Savior, the gateway to Eternal Life. As a believer in You, Lord, I stand on this promise of Salvation for those that are lost. Let my life be a guiding light that leads them straight to You. In Jesus' Name, Amen.

Saving Grace

Scripture

But when the kindness and love of God our Savior appeared, he saved us, not because of righteous things we had done, but because of his mercy. He saved us through the washing of rebirth and renewal by the Holy Spirit.

Titus 3:4-5

Scriptural Prayer

Oh Lord, I was unable to save myself. You choose and saved me with Your mercy, love, and amazing grace that changed my rebellious heart. My repentant heart delivered me to Your saving Salvation and made me anew. Hallelujah, I am Saved! In Jesus' Name, Amen.

Seeking God

Scripture

My heart says of you, "Seek his face!" Your face, LORD, I will seek.

Psalm 27:8

Scriptural Prayer

Heavenly Father, each day, I seek You in prayer and sing songs of praise to Your Holy name, in good times and in bad times. In times of trouble, my heart calls on Your name "Jesus." In times of celebrations, I call Your name "Jesus." In times of fear I call Your name "Jesus." In times of grief and sorrow I call Your name "Jesus." I seek You Jesus in all the things I do for You are my saving grace. There is no other name under heaven or on the earth that can save me. In Jesus' Name, Amen.

The Love of the Father

Scripture

Father, I want those you have given me to be with me where I am, and to see my glory, the glory you have given me because you loved me before the creation of the world.

John 17:24

Scriptural Prayer

Jesus, Son of God, I want to be with You in Your dwelling place because You loved me before I was created. Keep me in the palm of Your hand until You call me home to see Your glory. In Jesus' Name, Amen.

Trust

Scripture

I keep my eyes always on the LORD. With him at my right hand, I will not be shaken.

Psalm 16:8

Scriptural Prayer

Heavenly Father, as the ground shakes around me with unforeseen destruction from the voices of my enemies speaking loudly against me, I will stand firm, faithfully anchored, keeping my eyes upon You, the "Rock of my Salvation", who continues to intercede on my behalf. In Jesus' Name, Amen.

Spiritual

Growth

Abundantly Giving

Scripture

And God is able to bless you abundantly, so that in all things at all times, having all that you need, you will abound in every good work. Now he who supplies seed to the sower and bread for food will also supply and increase your store of seed and will enlarge the harvest of your righteousness.

2 Corinthians 9:8, 10

Scriptural Prayer

Heavenly Father, You have blessed me abundantly according to Your Word. Having all I need; I commit the works of my hands in thanksgiving to You for You have supplied my every need. I freely give as You have freely given to me. I thank You for increasing the fruits of my labor and giving me a humble heart to plant seeds of Your love and righteousness that will multiply the ministry for Your namesake. In Jesus' Name, Amen.

Accountable Living

Scripture

Now all has been heard; here is the conclusion of the matter: Fear God and keep his commandments, for this is the duty of all mankind.

Ecclesiastes 12:13

Scriptural Prayer

Heavenly Father, my obedience to Your commandments is in reverence of You! For all my deeds are seen and heard by You. Indeed, I will be held accountable for all my actions. Keep me accountable through the promptings of the Holy Spirit to live according to Your Word which confirms without a doubt that I am Your child. In Jesus' Name, Amen.

Control of the Tongue

Scripture

The soothing tongue is a tree of life, but a perverse tongue crushes the spirit.

Proverbs 15:4

Scripture Prayer

Heavenly Father show me when I am at the end of myself because I know that words do hurt. Give me the wisdom to know when to be silent. Place a guard at the lips of my mouth to keep peace and speak life only. I pray divine guidance by the Holy Spirit to be led by words of grace and not by my emotions. In Jesus' Name, Amen.

Direction of the Holy Spirit

Scripture

But when he, the Spirit of truth, comes, he will guide you into all the truth. He will not speak on his own; he will speak only what he hears, and he will tell you what is yet to come.

John 16:13

Scriptural Prayer

Heavenly Father, thank You, for the Spirit of Truth that guides me in Your truth. I will not allow the beliefs of man or worldly standards to determine my lifestyle. Reveal to me, by the leading of Your Spirit, the true way to go. In Jesus' Name, Amen.

Discerning Your Will

Scripture

The heart is deceitful above all things and beyond cure. Who can understand it? "I the LORD search the heart and examine the mind, to reward each person according to their conduct, according to what their deeds deserve."

Jeremiah 17:9-10

Scriptural Prayer

Oh Lord, You know the condition of my heart and the issues of life that flows from it. Jesus, guard my heart and my mind. Give me the discernment to know what Your Will is in every situation. Divinely connect my heart to Yours so that Your Holy Spirit will govern my life. In Jesus' Name, Amen.

Earthly Possessions That Hinder

Scripture

What good is it for someone to gain the whole world, yet forfeit their soul?

Mark 8:36

Scriptural Prayer

Heavenly Father, my soul is more valuable than all the riches of this world. Any worldly possession that hinders my relationship with You, reveal it and remove it for its temporary value may cause my separation from You. I will not forfeit my soul to the evils of counterfeit riches. In Jesus' Name, Amen.

Enduring Fruit

Scripture

You did not choose me, but I chose you and appointed you so that you might go and bear fruit—fruit that will last—and so that whatever you ask in my name the Father will give you.
John 15:16

Scriptural Prayer

Father God, thank You for choosing me and appointing me to represent Your Son, to be living proof of His lasting fruit of goodness, grace and enduring love that reflects who You are and guarantees Your blessings in that whatever I ask in Your name will be given to me. Let my life be a reflection of You forever. In Jesus' Name, Amen.

Evaluation of My Faults

Scripture

For God will bring every deed into judgment, including every hidden thing, whether it is good or evil.
Ecclesiastes 12:14

Scriptural Prayer

Heavenly Father open my eyes so that I may see my faults for there is nothing hidden from You. I submit myself to You. Help me to accept the true condition of my heart and remove every known and unknown evil motive that dwells within me. I want to be a living testimony that brings You glory and honor. In Jesus' Name, Amen.

Fasting

Scripture

Your fasting ends in quarreling and strife, and in striking each other with wicked fists. You cannot fast as you do today and expect your voice to be heard on high. Is not this the kind of fasting I have chosen: to loose the chains of injustice and untie the cords of the yoke, to set the oppressed free and break every yoke?

Isaiah 58:4, 6

Scriptural Prayer

Heavenly Father accept my time of consecration; let it not be in vain. In my secret place of prayer and fasting, clean me up and expose all my transgressions. Lord, accept this true submission of my human weaknesses. Strengthen me in Your Spirit to live according to Your Will, to be humble, and to live in peace with all mankind. In Jesus' Name, Amen.

Foolish Ways

Scripture

For the foolishness of God is wiser than human wisdom, and the weakness of God is stronger than human strength. Brothers and sisters, think of what you were when you were called. Not many of you were wise by human standards; not many were influential; not many were of noble birth. But God chose the foolish things of the world to shame the wise; God chose the weak things of the world to shame the strong. God chose the lowly things of this world and the despised things—and the things that are not—to nullify the things that are, so that no one may boast before him. It is because of him that you are in Christ Jesus, who has become for us wisdom from God—that is, our righteousness, holiness and redemption. Therefore, as it is written: "Let the one who boasts boast in the Lord."
1 Corinthians 1:25-31

Scriptural Prayer

Father God, thank You for using my foolish ways to teach me Your righteousness and choosing the lowly things of the world to shame the prideful. Therefore, I seek Your Word for knowledge and wisdom in understanding Your holiness and redemptive nature. According to Your Word, let my boasting be only in You because I am totally dependent on You. In Jesus' Name, Amen.

For Righteous Living

Scripture

Let us behave decently, as in the daytime, not in carousing and drunkenness, not in sexual immorality and debauchery, not in dissension and jealousy.

Romans 13:13

Scriptural Prayer

Heavenly Father, I see all the signs that confirms we are living in the end-times, and soon the call for judgment will arrive with life's recorded deeds. Does my behavior reflect that I am Your child? Lord, let Your truth examine my Christian walk. Reveal in my heart to accept and repent of any debauchery and wicked ways that resides within me hindering my living in the light of Your righteousness. In Jesus' Name, Amen.

Free from Worldly Thinking

Scripture

Set your minds on things above, not on earthly things. But now you must also rid yourselves of all such things as these: anger, rage, malice, slander, and filthy language from your lips.

Colossians 3:2, 8

Scriptural Prayer

Heavenly Father, I am a new creation in You with a renewed mind. I have been set free from the bondage of worldly thinking and unrighteous living. I will not go back! I will keep my mind on things pure allowing the Holy Spirit to govern my behavior and daily living. In Jesus' Name, Amen.

God's Undeniable Power

Scripture

For the LORD your God dried up the Jordan before you until you had crossed over. The LORD your God did to the Jordan what he had done to the Red Sea when he dried it up before us until we had crossed over. He did this so that all the peoples of the earth might know that the hand of the LORD is powerful and so that you might always fear the LORD your God."
Joshua 4:23-24

Scriptural Prayer

Lord, Your mighty acts of power and authority demonstrated for our forefathers are undeniable. I did not know how misguided and lost I was living in fear, but You removed the same obstacle of fear that had my forefathers bound. You have proven to me that there is nothing on earth, wickedness or afflictions, that is able to defeat Your power and authority. The reverence of Your power and authority has set me free from Satan's devices. I have crossed over by faith to my Lord and Savior. In Jesus' Name, Amen.

Godly Correction

Scripture

Have I now become your enemy by telling you the truth?
Galatians 4:16

Scriptural Prayer

Heavenly Father, Your truth brings correction and gives freedom from spiritual bondage. Help me not to be offended with those You have appointed to impart your Word of Truth when I am in error. Lord, help me to deliver the truth with words of grace in Your timing. Open my heart to receive your imparted Word of Truth with gratitude. Give me the understanding on how to apply it to my life. In Jesus' Name, Amen.

Greater Anointing

Scripture

'The glory of this present house will be greater than the glory of the former house,' says the LORD Almighty. 'And in this place I will grant peace,' declares the LORD Almighty."

Haggai 2:9

Scriptural Prayer

Lord Almighty, I pray for Your glory to be greater in our place of worship in these latter times and grant Your Spirit of peace to be with us now and forevermore. In Jesus Name, Amen.

Guidance

Scripture

You led your people like a flock by the hand of Moses and Aaron.

Psalm 77:20

Scriptural Prayer

Heavenly Father, just as You have led Moses and Aaron by the hand in the wilderness, lead me by Your Spirit down the path of life You have chosen for me and to fulfill Your divine purpose. In Jesus' Name, Amen.

Honoring Sabbath Day

Scripture

Observe my Sabbaths and have reverence for my sanctuary. I am the LORD.

Leviticus 26:2

Scriptural Prayer

Father God, You have given me unlimited access to the throne of grace. I will enter into your presence with total reverence of Your Holy Sanctuary, honoring the Sabbath Day as commanded. In Jesus' Name, Amen.

Making Good Choices

Scripture

Seek good, not evil, that you may live. Then the LORD God Almighty will be with you, just as you say he is.

Amos 5:14

Scriptural Prayer

Heavenly Father, I know that good and evil cannot commune together. I choose righteousness. I do not want to remove myself from Your protective presence with evil works. Let Your Spirit dwell in me and give me a pure heart that will produce a life of works that will bring You glory and honor forever. In Jesus' Name, Amen.

Meekness in Beauty

Scripture
Rather, it should be that of your inner self, the unfading beauty of a gentle and quiet spirit, which is of great worth in God's sight.
1 Peter 3:4

Scriptural Prayer
Heavenly Father let my outward appearance reflect who I am in You. Let my behavior and speech reflected Your unfading beauty and Your gentle, quiet Spirit which is valuable in Your sight. May it be evident to others that You live within my heart. In Jesus' Name, Amen.

New Beginnings

Scripture
Forget the former things; do not dwell on the past. See, I am doing a new thing! Now it springs up; do you not perceive it? I am making a way in the wilderness and streams in the wasteland.
Isaiah 43:18-19

Scriptural Prayer
Heavenly Father help me not to dwell on my past sins and sufferings but to focus on all the benefits guaranteed to me through Your Word. Thank you, for new beginnings. In Jesus' Name, Amen.

Our Nation

Scripture

I urge, then, first of all, that petitions, prayers, intercession and thanksgiving be made for all people for kings and all those in authority, that we may live peaceful and quiet lives in all godliness and holiness. This is good and pleases God our Savior.
1 Timothy 2:1-3

Scriptural Prayer

Heavenly Father, as the body of Christ comes together in prayer for our Nation, we pray for Your Will to be done on the Earth as it is in Heaven. We pray for repentance, unity, and humility towards all mankind. Father give our chosen leaders a Godly conscience to govern with biblical truths and peace. Thank You, for Your goodness and mercy that is upon our Nation. In Jesus' Name, Amen.

Praying Without Ceasing

Scripture

Pray continually.
1 Thessalonians 5:17

Scriptural Prayer

Heavenly Father, I will pray continuously for Your direction in every situation. I will wait in prayer for You to answer, and I will acknowledge You in my waiting. I will pray in faith and not doubt. I will not pray out of my fears, but I will pray with a strong, sound mind, trusting You for all my needs. In Jesus' Name, Amen.

Priority of Ministry

Scripture

Put your outdoor work in order and get your fields ready; after that, build your house.

Proverbs 24:27

Scripture Prayer

Heavenly Father instruct me how to prioritize the order of my ministry works according to Your divine purpose and timing. Lord, give me the wisdom to effectively manage the fields, your people, which are ready for harvest "to receive Your Word". Give me insight to Your blueprint for kingdom building. In Jesus' Name, Amen.

Reaping and Sowing

Scripture

The day of the LORD is near for all nations. As you have done, it will be done to you; your deeds will return upon your own head.

Obadiah 1:15

Scriptural Prayer

Heavenly Father, Your Word says I will reap what I sow. Show me the contents of my heart so that I do not deceive others or myself. For, I know all my actions will also be my fate. Lead me to be a doer of Your Word, living a life of charity and kindness towards all mankind. In Jesus' Name, Amen.

Safeguarding the Gospel in the Heart

Scripture

Guard the good deposit that was entrusted to you—guard it with the help of the Holy Spirit who lives in us.

2 Timothy 1:14

Scripture Prayer

Heavenly Father, I will guard Your biblical teachings of truth that is hidden in my heart. I will confirm every doctrine and teaching based on Your Holy Word and follow the leading of the Holy Spirit to discern what is true and rebuke what is false. In Jesus' Name, Amen.

Spiritual Discernment

Scripture

And no wonder, for Satan himself masquerades as an angel of light. It is not surprising, then, if his servants also masquerade as servants of righteousness. Their end will be what their actions deserve.

2 Corinthians 11:14-15

Scriptural Prayer

Heavenly Father, Your Word guarantees full exposure of every deceitful disguise of the enemy, and accountability will be served. Lord, give me spiritual discernment to see the evil plots of Satan and to know his deceitful ways. In Jesus' Name, Amen.

Spiritual Growth

Scripture

I gave you milk, not solid food, for you were not yet ready for it. Indeed, you are still not ready. You are still worldly. For since there is jealousy and quarreling among you, are you not worldly? Are you not acting like mere humans?

1 Corinthians 3:2-3

Scriptural Prayer

Heavenly Father, it is time for me to grow up and to mature spiritually in the things of You. Help me to put away the things that easily entangle me to react based on my feelings, like a child having temper tantrums. Lord, lead me by Your Spirit to live according to Your Word, to be mature in You, and to be spiritually strong, not easily moved by worldly desires and conflicts, but to have a humble heart that desires to fulfill Your Will and to be effective for kingdom building. In Jesus' Name, Amen.

Spiritual Unity

Scripture

Make every effort to keep the unity of the Spirit through the bond of peace.

Ephesians 4:3

Scriptural Prayer

Heavenly Father keep me in sync with the Holy Spirit and let Your peace guide me in times of discord. In Jesus' Name, Amen.

Stability

Scripture

Commit to the LORD whatever you do, and he will establish your plans.

Proverbs 16:3

Scriptural Prayer

Heavenly Father, I am committed to doing what You have called me to do. I will always seek You first because You pre-ordained the plans for my life. Peace, joy, hope, and love journeys with me as You establish me for Your purpose. I will offer my life as a living sacrifice that will bring honor and glory to You. In Jesus' Name, Amen.

Stewardship in Ministry

Scripture

Keep watch over yourselves and all the flock of which the Holy Spirit has made you overseers. Be shepherds of the church of God, which he bought with his own blood.

Acts 20:28

Scriptural Prayer

Heavenly Father help me to be a good steward to those You have given to me in the ministry for they have been bought with the precious blood of Your Son. Keep me spiritually alert, physically, and mentally strong with the power of the Holy Spirit, to stand in unity with my brothers and sisters in Christ defeating evil. In Jesus' Name, Amen.

Stillness

Scripture

Do not be quick with your mouth, do not be hasty in your heart to utter anything before God. God is in heaven and you are on earth, so let your words be few. **Ecclesiastes 5:2**

Scriptural Prayer

Heavenly Father, I take the position of quietness before You to listen in silence, calming my thoughts. 'Because You know' I will wait on you to settle the issues of my heart. In Jesus' Name, Amen.

Strengthen Your Faith

Scripture

But you, dear friends, by building yourselves up in your most holy faith and praying in the Holy Spirit, keep yourselves in God's love as you wait for the mercy of our Lord Jesus Christ to bring you to eternal life.
Jude 1:20-21

Scriptural Prayer

Heavenly Father, I pray in the Holy Spirit to build up my faith in these times of uncertainties. Keep my faith rooted in the power of Your love and mercy. In Jesus' Name, Amen.

The Goodness of God Within Me

Scripture

For it is God who works in you to will and to act in order to fulfill his good purpose. **Philippians 2:13**

Scriptural Prayer

Heavenly Father, I know that all the good things I do and speak are because Your Spirit lives within me. Keep me mindful and sensitive by your Spirit to live according to Your Word and to fulfill Your purpose for me. In Jesus' Name, Amen.

Submission to His Will

Scripture

He has shown you, O mortal, what is good. And what does the LORD require of you? To act justly and to love mercy and to walk humbly with your God.
Micah 6:8

Scriptural Prayer

Heavenly Father, You have shown me through Your Word, what is required of me as Your child, which is to be humble, to do what is good, and to live justly, full of mercy and love towards all. Continue to transform my human nature to model after You. In Jesus' Name, Amen.

Wisdom, Understanding and Knowledge

Scripture
Who gives the ibis wisdom or gives the rooster understanding?
Job 38:36

Scriptural Prayer
Heavenly Father, You are the giver of wisdom and understanding. Even the rooster understands to obey Your command of when to crow. Lord, I pray that You give me that same wisdom and understanding to obey Your commands and the knowledge how to apply Your Word to my life. In Jesus' Name, Amen.

Wise Living

Scripture
Be very careful, then, how you live—not as unwise but as wise. Therefore do not be foolish, but understand what the Lord's will is.
Ephesians 5:15, 17

Scriptural Prayer
Heavenly Father, I have learned through life's experiences that my foolish and selfish desires only gave me temporary fulfillment. Let me walk in the wisdom of Your Word of truth so that my life and my speech reflect my transformation in You. In Jesus' Name, Amen.

Relationships

Children Safety

Scripture

For it is written: He will command his angels concerning you to guard you carefully.

Luke 4:10

Scriptural Prayer

Heavenly Father keep all our children safe as they travel to and from school. Protect them in the classrooms, on the playgrounds, on the athletic fields, in the restrooms and in the cafeterias. Guard them from all harm, danger, and bullying. Guide the teachers and school staff to speak words of life and affirmation to our children. May no child come to or leave school hungry, neglected, or abused. As parents, let us be committed to ensure that no child is left behind. In Jesus' Name, Amen.

Disarming Conflict

Scripture

A gentle answer turns away wrath, but a harsh word stirs up anger.

Proverbs 15:1

Scriptural Prayer

Heavenly Father let Your peace that dwells within me be the peace I speak in times of conflict. Give me the words that will disarm the noise of confusion and hostility. Reveal the truth that allows the matter to be settled permanently and peacefully. In Jesus' Name, Amen.

Divine Order

Scripture

For God is not a God of disorder but of peace—as in all the congregations of the Lord's people.

1 Corinthians 14:33

Scriptural Prayer

Heavenly Father, You established in the beginning divine order and authority. Without Your divine order our marriages, families, churches, schools, and workplaces will be overtaken with chaos and confusion, which is not of You. Give me the discernment not to fall into the trap of man's perception of order which goes against Your Word, for where there is no order there is no peace; where there is no peace there is no God. In Jesus' Name, Amen.

Edification

Scripture

The eyes of the LORD are everywhere, keeping watch on the wicked and the good.

Proverbs 15:3

Scriptural Prayer

Lord, nothing is hidden from You because You see all good and evil that is in the earth. My secret motives and hidden acts are clearly seen by You. Cleanse my heart from all unrighteousness and use me to be a blessing of good works towards others. Fill my mouth with words that edifies the hearer and honors You. Keep me mindful in well doing for Your namesake. In Jesus' Name, Amen.

Exposing Deceit

Scripture

I say this because many deceivers, who do not acknowledge Jesus Christ as coming in the flesh, have gone out into the world. Any such person is the deceiver and the antichrist.

2 John 1:7

Scriptural Prayer

Heavenly Father, I will follow Your commands and write them on the tablets of my heart. I know Your biblical truths will guide and protect me from deceivers and false doctrines, which speak and teach against Your Word. Confirm Your Word by the leading of the Holy Spirit and expose all lies spoken against Your Word. In Jesus' Name, Amen.

Family Servitude

Scripture

Now be pleased to bless the house of your servant, that it may continue forever in your sight; for you, Sovereign LORD, have spoken, and with your blessing the house of your servant will be blessed forever.

2 Samuel 7:29

Scriptural Prayer

Sovereign Lord, our family welcomes Your holy presence to dwell in our hearts and in our homes. Our hearts are unified on one accord to serve and love You forever. Bless our home as we continue to honor You by living according to Your Word. In Jesus' Name, Amen.

For the Elderly

Scripture

Even to your old age and gray hairs I am he, I am he who will sustain you. I have made you and I will carry you; I will sustain you and I will rescue you.

Isaiah 46:4

Scriptural Prayer

Heavenly Father, thank You for Your sweet, tender, merciful, and compassionate care for the elderly, who are unable to care for themselves and for those who are living in nursing faculties. Thank You, for Your promises of reassurance that You are a sustainer and rescuer in their times of need. In Jesus' Name, Amen.

Forgiveness

Scripture

Shouldn't you have had mercy on your fellow servant just as I had on you?

Matthew 18:33

Scriptural Prayer

Heavenly Father, according to Your Word, I am to forgive my debtors as You have forgiven me of my debts and transgressions. Remove any excuses or selfish motives that hinders me from releasing others of their transgressions against me. In Jesus' Name, Amen.

Forgiveness and Love

Scripture

Bear with each other and forgive one another if any of you has a grievance against someone. Forgive as the Lord forgave you.
Colossians 3:13

Scriptural Prayer

Heavenly Father, thank You, for Your endless love and forgiveness. I desire to be more Christ-like in sharing the same love and forgiveness to others that You have shown me. Help me to be quick to forgive others bearing them up in love. In Jesus' Name, Amen.

Godly Influence

Scripture

In the name of the Lord Jesus Christ, we command you, brothers and sisters, to keep away from every believer who is idle and disruptive and does not live according to the teaching you received from us.
2 Thessalonians 3:6

Scriptural Prayer

Heavenly Father let me not be influence by those who are idolatrous, disruptive, and whose lifestyle do not reflect Christian values. Let my Christian walk be a reflection of Your love that draws them to You. In Jesus' Name, Amen.

Grateful Nation

Scripture

Who will not fear you, Lord, and bring glory to your name? For you alone are holy. All nations will come and worship before you, for your righteous acts have been revealed.
Revelation 15:4

Scriptural Prayer

Holy, Holy, Holy is Your name declared by the angels in the heavenly realms for they recognize Your mighty power to deliver us from wrath. We as Your people stand as a nation with hands lifted up, proclaim you, Lord, Holy, Holy, Holy. Oh Lord, receive our prayers of repentance. By Your spoken Word, reconcile us back to Your Glory, and awaken the hearts of Your people for Salvation's sake. In Jesus' Name, Amen.

Loving Others

Scripture

The commandments, "You shall not commit adultery," "You shall not murder," "You shall not steal," "You shall not covet," and whatever other command there may be, are summed up in this one command: "Love your neighbor as yourself."
Romans 13:9

Scriptural Prayer

Heavenly Father help me to fulfill the law of Your Commandments. Give me the character to love others as myself. If, I have any deficiencies of love, expose it, and heal me. Lord, give me the fortitude to mend broken relationships and a heart of love living in obedience according to Your commands. In Jesus' Name, Amen.

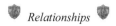

Lying Lips and Deceit

Scripture
Save me, LORD, from lying lips and from deceitful tongues.
Psalm 120:2

Scriptural Prayer
Heavenly Father, if I cannot speak truth with honesty then seal my mouth and bridle my tongue. Save me from those who speak lies and slander my name. Lord reveal the truth and let the words that I speak affirm your truths. In Jesus' Name, Amen.

Marriage

Scripture
Therefore what God has joined together, let no one separate.
Mark 10:9

Scriptural Prayer
Heavenly Father, I thank You for the bond of marriage. It is more than a written contract. It is a blood covenant between You, Man, and Woman. It is a sacrament of holy joining that no one should separate. Lord, I give my sacred bond of love to You and to my soul mate forevermore. In Jesus' Name, Amen.

Protection for Missionaries

Scripture

My prayer is not that you take them out of the world but that you protect them from the evil one. As you sent me into the world, I have sent them into the world.

John 17:15, 18

Scriptural Prayer

Jesus, I declare Your spoken prayer in John 17:15, for divine protection over our brothers and sisters in Christ whom You have sanctify and sent out into the world. Be their fortress and keep them from all harm. Preserve their lives from the evil works of Satan as they continue to do Your Will in the earth. In Jesus' Name, Amen.

Rearing Your Children in Christ

Scripture

Fathers, do not exasperate your children; instead, bring them up in the training and instruction of the Lord.

Ephesians 6:4

Scriptural Prayer

Heavenly Father, it is my obligation as a parent to bring my children up in the knowledge of You, teaching my child with patience and love. Lord, give me Your insight to teach with humility and encouragement that leads to excellence in their learning. Let Your joy fill their hearts in all the things they achieve according to Your purpose for their lives. In Jesus' Name, Amen.

The Broken-hearted

Scripture

A happy heart makes the face cheerful, but heartache crushes the spirit.

Proverbs 15:13

Scriptural Prayer

Heavenly Father keep me sensitive to those who are broken in spirit for only You know the true sufferings of others. I will joyfully share my testimony of Your amazing grace and Your healing power to the broken hearted. In Jesus' Name, Amen.

To Love My Enemies

Scripture

But love your enemies, do good to them, and lend to them without expecting to get anything back. Then your reward will be great, and you will be children of the Most High, because he is kind to the ungrateful and wicked.

Luke 6:35

Scriptural Prayer

Heavenly Father let me not react negatively to those who despise me but help me respond with kindness, for all my actions come with great reward in You. Give me the grace to hold my peace and to remain blameless in my Christian walk with You. In Jesus' Name, Amen.

Wise Counsel

Scripture
There is no wisdom, no insight, no plan that can succeed against the LORD.
Proverbs 21:30

Scriptural Prayer
Oh Lord, nothing can stand against You. I seek Your counsel and Your plans for me because there is no one wiser than You! You established the foundations of the world and the comings and goings of mankind are not hidden from You. There is no understanding that surpasses You! In Jesus' Name, Amen.

Overcoming

Adversity

Addiction

Scripture

Wine is a mocker and beer a brawler; whoever is led astray by them is not wise.

Proverbs 20:1

Scriptural Prayer

Heavenly Father, an addiction can be any substance that defiles my body and causes me to be out of control. Remove the taste and the desires of self-indulging addictions by killing the root cause that leads me to overindulge and justify my actions. Lord, open my heart to the truth to recognize and accept my weakness, and give me the courage to walk away from it! In Jesus' Name, Amen.

Avenge Wickedness

Scripture

Away from me, all you who do evil, for the LORD has heard my weeping. The LORD has heard my cry for mercy; the LORD accepts my prayer. All my enemies will be overwhelmed with shame and anguish; they will turn back and suddenly be put to shame.

Psalm 6:8-10

Scriptural Prayer

Oh Lord, you heard my cries of mercy and exposed the sinful exploits of my enemies who pursue me to do evil against me. Oh Lord, I declare You are greater than my fears. I stand in awe for You heard my prayer; suddenly my enemies fled with shame and anguish the moment they denied You. In Jesus' Name, Amen.

Being Victorious During Trials

Scripture

For everyone born of God overcomes the world. This is the victory that has overcome the world, even our faith. Who is it that overcomes the world? Only the one who believes that Jesus is the Son of God.

1 John 5:4-5

Scriptural Prayer

Heavenly Father, I am Your child! I am an overcomer through Your Son, Jesus Christ, my Savior. Because He overcame the world and conquered death victoriously with all power in His hands, I too will overcome the trials and tribulations that are before me by the blood of Jesus Christ. In Jesus' Name, Amen.

Deliverance

Scripture

And the LORD changed the wind to a very strong west wind, which caught up the locusts and carried them into the Red Sea. Not a locust was left anywhere in Egypt.

Exodus 10:19

Scriptural Prayer

Oh Lord, Your spoken Word exposes all deceit, changing the events of my enemy's evil plots. You tossed deadly plagues into the deepest sea that was assigned to kill me. You heard my cries and made a way of escape for me. Thank You, Almighty Lord, for rescuing and delivering me from all evil. In Jesus' Name, Amen.

Deliverance from Anger

Scripture

"In your anger do not sin": Do not let the sun go down while you are still angry, and do not give the devil a foothold.
Ephesians 4:26-27

Scriptural Prayer

Heavenly Father, let there be no sin found in my anger, but let me be quick to release it by closing the door on the devil's traps of un-forgiveness and bitterness that may be harboring within me. Let my confession of repentance expose the devil's tactics and give me a heart for forgiveness and a peace of mind. In Jesus' Name, Amen.

Deliverance from My Enemy

Scripture

I love you, LORD, my strength. The LORD is my rock, my fortress and my deliverer; my God is my rock, in whom I take refuge, my shield and the horn of my salvation, my stronghold.
Psalm 18:1-2

Scriptural Prayer

Lord, Your divine presence is a wall of protection; Your watchful eye guides me with victory disarming the evil plots assigned to destroy me. Your Holy Word is my guidepost of truth. Your redemptive power restores me back to Your amazing grace; and through my confession of faith, I am delivered and made spiritually stronger. Your Agape love rescues me. Father, my love is Yours forever. In Jesus' Name, Amen.

Healing

Scripture

Then he said to me, "Prophesy to the breath; prophesy, son of man, and say to it, 'This is what the Sovereign LORD says: Come, breath, from the four winds and breathe into these slain, that they may live.'" So I prophesied as he commanded me, and breath entered them; they came to life and stood up on their feet a vast army.

Ezekiel 37:9-10

Scriptural Prayer

Heavenly Father, according to the authority that You gave Ezekiel in the Valley of Dry Bones to speak life, with that same God given authority, I command healing in (Insert person's name) body. I command in Jesus' name that this attack to their body (Name the condition) to line-up with God's healing Word and His Will for their life to be fully restored. You are healed. In Jesus' Name, Amen.

Patience for the Hurting

Scripture

A person's wisdom yields patience; it is to one's glory to overlook an offense.

Proverbs 19:11

Scriptural Prayer:

Heavenly Father, as I mature in You, I understand the importance of being patient, quick to listen, and slow to speak. Lord, help me to understand the reactions of hurting people and not to be offended. Help me to speak words of grace, hope, and encouragement that wins them over to You. In Jesus' Name, Amen.

Peaceful Sleep

Scripture

In peace I will lie down and sleep, for you alone, LORD, make me dwell in safety.

Psalm 4:8

Scriptural Prayer

Heavenly Father, Your blessed assurance of peaceful sleep covers me like a divine cloak of protection. Your living power and continuous presence calms, restores, and brings new life to my body and mind in my quiet state of rest and sleep. By Your mighty commands, I am safely kept from all harm and danger. Sovereign Lord, thank You for the gift of inner peace that leads to peaceful sleep in You. In Jesus' Name, Amen.

Prevailing Against Temptation

Scripture

Because he himself suffered when he was tempted, he is able to help those who are being tempted.

Hebrews 2:18

Scriptural Prayer

Heavenly Father, knowing that Your Son suffered while being tempted without sinning gives me the strength to resist all forms of temptation. May my faith prevail during times of suffering through the power of Your Spirit. In Jesus' Name, Amen.

Rescue

Scripture

This is what the LORD says: "Stand at the crossroads and look; ask for the ancient paths, ask where the good way is, and walk in it, and you will find rest for your souls. But you said, 'We will not walk in it.'

Jeremiah 6:16

Scriptural Prayer

Oh Lord, I was warned. I had a choice. I deliberately refused Your way. I followed my own desires and pride that led me by the way of destruction and shame. My eyes are weary and consumed with tears. My heart repents; Lord rescue me. I will stand still in prayer and wait to walk the pathway you have chosen for me to follow which is the good and righteous way. When I follow the righteous way, my soul rests, and I am secure in You. In Jesus' Name, Amen.

Steadfastness in Trials

Scripture

Blessed is the one who perseveres under trial because, having stood the test, that person will receive the crown of life that the Lord has promised to those who love him.

James 1:12

Scriptural Prayer

Heavenly Father, thank You for Your promises of victory and eternal Salvation for those who love You. When adversities come in like flood, help me to stand strong during my test to receive my crown of victory at the end of the trial. In Jesus' Name, Amen.

Strengthened to Overcome

Scripture

Because he himself suffered when he was tempted, he is able to help those who are being tempted.
Hebrews 2:18

Scriptural Prayer

Heavenly Father, Your Son Jesus suffered and overcame temptation, and by the power of the Holy Spirit, I too will overcome my human weaknesses and trials. Thank You, for being my way of escape. In Jesus' Name, Amen.

Temper

Scripture

A hot-tempered person stirs up conflict, but the one who is patient calms a quarrel. **Proverbs 15:18**

Scriptural Prayer

Oh Lord anoint me with Your Spirit of peace and sound mind. When adversities attack causing great discord, touch my tongue with words of grace. Pour into my heart your mercy of love as I declare Your Word, blessed are "the Peacemakers: for they shall be called the Children of God." I am Your child! In Jesus' Name, Amen.

The Weak in Faith

Scripture
Be merciful to those who doubt; save others by snatching them from the fire; to others show mercy, mixed with fear—hating even the clothing stained by corrupted flesh.
Jude 1:22-23

Scriptural Prayer
Oh Lord let my testimony of Your Son, Jesus Christ, build others up in their faith, strengthening them where they are weak, and bring hope to the hurting and insight to those who are lost and seeking Your Salvation. In Jesus' Name, Amen.

The Lord's Prayer

Our Father which art in heaven, Hallowed be your name.
Thy kingdom come, Thy will be done in earth, as it is in
heaven.
Give us this day our daily bread.
And forgive us our debts, as we forgive our debtors.
And lead us not into temptation, but deliver us from evil:
For thine is the kingdom, and the power, and the glory,
forever. Amen.
Matthew 6:9-13 King James Version

Date Prayed: Date Answered:

Prayer Log

Date and write out your prayer request. When your prayer is
answered, record the date, and rejoice.

Date Prayed: Date Answered:

Prayer Log

Date and write out your prayer request. When your prayer is
answered, record the date, and rejoice.

Date Prayed: Date Answered:

_____   _____

Prayer Log

Date and write out your prayer request. When your prayer is
answered, record the date, and rejoice.

_____

_____

_____

_____

_____

_____

_____

_____

_____

_____

_____

Date Prayed: Date Answered:

_____   _____

Prayer Log

Date and write out your prayer request. When your prayer is
answered, record the date, and rejoice.

_____

_____

_____

_____

_____

_____

_____

_____

_____

_____

_____

Date Prayed: Date Answered:

Prayer Log

Date and write out your prayer request. When your prayer is
answered, record the date, and rejoice.

Date Prayed: Date Answered:

_____   _____

Prayer Log

Date and write out your prayer request. When your prayer is
answered, record the date, and rejoice.

_____

_____

_____

_____

_____

_____

_____

_____

_____

_____

_____

_____

Date Prayed: Date Answered:

Prayer Log

Date and write out your prayer request. When your prayer is
answered, record the date, and rejoice.

_____

_____

_____

_____

_____

_____

_____

_____

_____

_____

_____

Date Prayed: Date Answered:

_____   _____

Prayer Log

Date and write out your prayer request. When your prayer is
answered, record the date, and rejoice.

_____

_____

_____

_____

_____

_____

_____

_____

_____

_____

_____

_____

Date Prayed: Date Answered:

_____   _____

Prayer Log

Date and write out your prayer request. When your prayer is
answered, record the date, and rejoice.

_____

_____

_____

_____

_____

_____

_____

_____

_____

_____

_____

Date Prayed: Date Answered:

Prayer Log

Date and write out your prayer request. When your prayer is
answered, record the date, and rejoice.

Date Prayed: Date Answered:

Prayer Log

Date and write out your prayer request. When your prayer is
answered, record the date, and rejoice.

Date Prayed: Date Answered:

Prayer Log

Date and write out your prayer request. When your prayer is
answered, record the date, and rejoice.

_____

_____

_____

_____

_____

_____

_____

_____

_____

_____

_____

Date Prayed: Date Answered:

Prayer Log

Date and write out your prayer request. When your prayer is
answered, record the date, and rejoice.

_____

_____

_____

_____

_____

_____

_____

_____

_____

_____

_____

Date Prayed: Date Answered:

_____   _____

Prayer Log

Date and write out your prayer request. When your prayer is
answered, record the date, and rejoice.

_____

_____

_____

_____

_____

_____

_____

_____

_____

_____

_____

_____

Date Prayed: Date Answered:

Prayer Log

Date and write out your prayer request. When your prayer is
answered, record the date, and rejoice.

_____

_____

_____

_____

_____

_____

_____

_____

_____

_____

Made in the USA
Columbia, SC
01 September 2020

17399319R00062